NOTTINGHAM
EVENING
POST

Images of Nottinghamshire

**NOTTINGHAM
EVENING
POST**

Nottinghamshire

Images of

Breedon Books
Publishing Company
Derby

First published in Great Britain by
The Breedon Books Publishing Company Limited
44 Friar Gate, Derby, DE1 1DA.
1995

ISBN 1 875983 034 X

Printed and bound by
Butler & Tanner Ltd, Caxton Road, Frome, Somerset.

Cover printed by
Premier Print, Ilkeston Road, Nottingham.

Colour separations by
Colour Services, Leicester.

Contents

Introduction

NOTTINGHAMSHIRE has been called The County With Everything. There is so much to do and to see that the tourist is spoiled for choice.

You cannot escape the influence of Robin Hood – in the historic city of Nottingham, in the 450 remaining acres of Sherwood Forest and in many towns and villages whose history is associated with the legendary outlaw.

At Papplewick, for instance, there were many clashes with Robin's Merry Men,

The remains of 70,000-year-old cave homes at Creswell Crags, which cavemen hewed out of limestone in prehistoric times.

for it was the base of the dreaded wardens who enforced the laws of the royal hunting forest.

It was here, at the Church of St James, on the edge of the village, that Robin rescued Ellen from a wedding to an ageing knight so that she could marry one of the outlaw's trusty followers, Alan A'Dale.

Robin, himself, is said to have married Maid Marian at the Church of St Mary, Edwinstowe. Fountaindale, near Mansfield, was the scene of the famed river fight between Robin and Friar Tuck.

And King John's Palace, once a royal hunting lodge, lies in ruins at old Clipstone, little more than a stone's throw from Blidworth where, legend has it, Will Scarlet is buried in the churchyard.

Robin Hood has brought world fame to Nottinghamshire but there is so much more to the county, with its natural beauty, rich historic heritage and importance as the home of industrial pioneers, literary giants and leading religious figures of the past.

The stocking frame, the world's first knitting machine, was invented at Calverton by the Revd William Lee in 1589; romantic poet Lord Byron lived at Newstead Abbey, controversial author D.H.Lawrence hailed from Eastwood; religious leaders Archbishop Cranmer, who wrote the Book of Common Prayer, George Fox, the power behind the Quaker movement and John and Charles Wesley, founders of Methodism, all lived in Nottinghamshire.

William Booth from Sneinton started the Salvation Army in Nottingham and the Pilgrim Fathers Movement, which went on to shape the destiny of the United States, was founded in Babworth and Scrooby.

Industry in Nottinghamshire is diverse. Apart from textiles and lace, for which it is renowned, it was a leading centre in coal-mining's heyday, is famous for its tobacco, pharmaceuticals and cycle

A memorial to John Wesley, one of the founders of Methodism, who was born in Epworth on 17 June 1705.

industries, important for the mineral gypsum, a centre for brewing and with a fine tradition of farming. Laxton is the only village in Europe to maintain the medieval open field system of farming.

Nottinghamshire has a great sporting tradition, not least in soccer, with a Premier League club, Nottingham Forest; the world's oldest League club, Notts County, and a third League club Mansfield Town.

It has a famous Test ground, Trent Bridge, home of Nottinghamshire County Cricket Club, a well-known rugby football club, Nottingham, two horse-racing tracks, Nottingham and Southwell, and a top ice-hockey team, Nottingham Panthers. The National Water Sports Centre is at Holme Pierrepont.

A tour of the towns and villages is as educational as it is interesting; as rewarding as it is uplifting.

All-in-all, it is a wonderful county to visit. And second to none as a place in which to live, facts which reflect great credit on the vision and clear-thinking of both the County and City Councils.

The Major Oak in Sherwood Forest at Edwinstowe – the mighty tree is said to have been the hiding place of Robin Hood and some of his merry men.

Newstead Abbey and Lord Byron

THE dashing Lord Byron, the most charismatic of all English poets, inherited his title, along with Newstead Abbey, when he was only ten years old from 'the Wicked Lord', his great uncle the 5th Lord Byron.

But it was a mixed blessing because the rare medieval priory, the Byron family seat, with 300 acres of what are now magnificent grounds was in a derelict state.

In fact, although Byron's mother brought him to Nottinghamshire in 1798, they could not live in the derelict abbey and, instead, the family was forced to rent rooms in St James's Street near Nottingham Castle, moving later to Burgage Manor in Southwell.

His vacations from first Harrow and then Cambridge were spent there and he was a regular visitor to the Assembly Rooms (now part of the Saracen's Head Hotel) and Southwell Minster.

Byron moved into Newstead in 1809 when he came of age, and was soon bringing glamour to the abbey but also wild parties, scandal and intrigue.

He took his seat in the House of Lords that year before leaving for long periods abroad.

Fugitive Pieces, Byron's first collection of poems, was printed by Ridges of Market Place, Newark, where one of his ancestors was Governor during the Civil War.

But he achieved fame with *Cantos I and II* of *Childe Harold's Pilgrimage* in March 1812, and became the idol of London, chased, among others, by Lady Caroline Lamb, who with some justification, saw him as 'mad, bad and dangerous to know', although she was unstable herself.

Somehow, Byron managed to combine a crazy social life with prolific writing.

Scandal came over his relationship with his half-sister Augusta Leigh, daughter of his father Mad Jack's first marriage.

When his short marriage to Annabella Milbanke broke up, predictably, in 1816, the disgraced Byron, deep in debt, left England for good.

Byron sold Newstead Abbey in 1818, solving his financial problems at a stroke and went on to write his crowning jewel, the lengthy poem *Don Juan*.

He died of fever in Missolonghi, in April 1924, a hero in the eyes of the people of Greece. His body was returned to Nottinghamshire and he lies in Hucknall Church.

To this day, the ghost of the White Lady is said to walk through Newstead Abbey Park. The daughter of one of the estate's dog keepers, she was killed by a carrier's cart in Nottingham.

The face that made a thousand hearts flutter – Lord Byron in his prime.

A corner of Newstead Abbey in 1836.

The Prime Minister of Greece, M.Venizelos, raises his hat to the crowd outside Nottingham Council House after handing over Newstead Abbey to Nottingham City Council in July 1931.

The terrace, Annesley Hall, a favourite walk of Mary Chaworth and Byron, pictured in 1924. In the foreground is the door which Byron pierced with bullets.

The Parish Church of St. Mary Magdalene, Hucknall

The Funeral of Lord Noel Byron

The Byron Vault

Jim Bettridge, then caretaker of Hucknall Parish Church, with his book on Byron, which he had published when he was 80, in January 1971. He described seeing Byron's well-preserved body, which had been embalmed in Greece 114 years earlier, after the coffin arrived at the church.

Members of Blidworth Adult Education class, based at Rainworth, painting and sketching during a field trip to Newstead Abbey in May 1972.

Lawrence, The Controversial Moralist

THE landscapes of Nottinghamshire are vividly brought to life in the work of Eastwood-born D.H.Lawrence (1885-1930), the first major working-class novelist, hugely controversial but a moralist despite his monumental clashes with the decency laws.

The son of a coal-miner and a former schoolteacher, David Herbert Lawrence developed from a sickly child into one of the great novelists.

He was born on 11 September 1885, and although the family of seven moved to various houses in Eastwood during his childhood, he was always inspired by the local countryside.

Lawrence, spurred on by his mother but with no encouragement from his father, won a scholarship to Nottingham High School. Sadly, he had to leave when he was 15 to help supplement the family's meagre income.

He joined Haywood's surgical appliance factory in Nottingham, working there for only three months before going down with pneumonia, from which he nearly died.

Later, he worked as an unqualified teacher at the British School, Eastwood, going on to University College, Nottingham, where he gained his teaching certificate.

He moved to Croydon to teach but by 1912, though in poor health, he had had his first novel, *The White Peacock*, published and was working on *Sons and Lovers*, published the following year. By now he had broken off his engagement to Louie Burrows, whom he met at Ilkeston Pupil Teacher Centre in 1903.

He returned to Eastwood but eloped to Germany with mother of three, Frieda, wife of Professor Ernest Weekley of Mapperley. He married Frieda two years later.

His masterpiece *The Rainbow*, set in Cossall, was seized by police when it was published in 1915 as being obscene and the sequel to this, *Women in Love*, though completed the following year, was not published until 1921 because British publishers declined to take it on.

He lived in England until 1919, when he went abroad again with his wife, eventually settling in Italy, where he wrote prolifically as well as developing an interest in painting.

It was there he wrote his final and most controversial novel, *Lady Chatterley's Lover*, set in the East Midlands, which was printed privately in Italy in 1928. Lawrence died in Vence, near Venice in March 1930, aged only 44.

D.H.Lawrence
– a study
taken in 1906.

D.H.Lawrence's birthplace in Victoria
Street, Eastwood.

The parlour in the Lawrence's home.

Filming at Bagthorpe in April 1980, of Sons and Lovers, *for a six-part television series.*

Riddings Band, under bandmaster Wilf Saint, rehearse their piece for the television series. They include Ron and Kevin Saint, Chris Cumberland, Stuart Lacey, Ron Fisher, Neil Willcockson, Jim Wayne, Mark Hanson, Ron Fisher, Kevin Aldred and John Webb.

Sculptor Diana Thomson with her six-foot bronze statue of D.H.Lawrence being delivered to Nottingham University for display at the School of Education in June 1993.

Home of the Bramley Apple

THE Bramley apple originates from Southwell and the very first tree, dating back nearly 190 years is still producing quality fruit weighing up to a pound-and-a-half.

Nancy Harrison, who bought the garden where it grows and the derelict cottage that went with it more than 30 years ago, has looked after the tree ever since.

The original trunk, blown down in a gale, lies on the ground with a secondary trunk growing from it.

Mary-Ann Brailsford, the daughter of the family then living at the cottage, grew the tree from pips planted in 1809 when she was a child.

After her parents died, Mary-Ann continued to live there with her sister until 1838.

Eight years later, local innkeeper and butcher Matthew Bramley bought the cottage and in 1856 nurseryman Henry Merryweather, impressed by the quality, taste and size of Matthew's apples, was given permission to grow grafts from the tree and to market the fruit.

A condition was that the apple should bear Mr Bramley's name.

The variety was formally recognised by the Royal Horticultural Society as Bramley's Seedling in 1876, 14 years after the fruit was first sold.

The Merryweather nursery is still going strong, run by Roger, Henry's great-grandson. A Bramley Museum was created there by the Bramley Campaign Group in 1990.

Today, around 130,000 tonnes of Bramley apples are marketed every year.

As cooking apples, they are the best. And there is a bonus – they are delightful eaters when ripe.

The first Bramley apple tree ablaze with blossom in May 1962.

Bramley Tree Cottage, home of Matthew Bramley, who grew the first Bramley apple tree, pictured in 1929.

The Splendour of Wollaton Hall

WOLLATON Hall was completed in 1588, the year of the Spanish Armada. The Italianate-style mansion cost Sir Francis Willoughby £80,000 and took eight years to build on the 774-acre grounds. Stone for building the hall was brought by packhorse from Ancaster. The Central Hall is 50ft high, with windows 35ft above floor level. But little of the Elizabethan interior remains. The Willoughby family owned the estate for 600 years. Sir Hugh Willoughby, the famous seaman, was frozen to death in 1554 while attempting to find the North-West Passage to India. Lord Middleton, a Willoughby, sold the mansion to Nottingham Corporation in September 1924, for £200,000. The following March his Wollaton and Ilkeston estates were purchased by the Corporation for £243,000. King George V had lunch in the hall during a visit to Nottingham before the outbreak of World War One. There was never a bathroom at the hall, although hardy guests were free to take an icy dip in an underground reservoir.

Wollaton Hall pictured during the harsh winter of 1947.

Wollaton Hall takes on new look under floodlight in June 1988.

This huge horse-gin, c.1844, used at Longton Colliery, Pinxton, to haul miners up and down the lift shaft, was given to Nottingham's Industrial Museum, Wollaton Park, by the NCB.

Rometheus Healing With The Power of Fire, *one of the murals at Wollaton Park.*

The Royal Canadian Air Force Pipe Band in the 1953 Coronation Tattoo at Wollaton Park.

This sheepdog is a study in concentration during the City of Nottingham Show at Wollaton Park in 1985.

This Nottingham-built 1935 Brough Superior Dual Purpose car was loaned to the Industrial Museum at Wollaton Park in February 1985. The motorcycle is a 1921 Brough Superior. The firm supplied seven of its motorcycles to Lawrence of Arabia.

The cast of a pageant in 1953 in Wollaton Park.

Royal Visits to Nottinghamshire

A guard of honour of Boy Scouts lines up for the arrival of King George V at Welbeck Abbey in December 1912.

*The Duchess of York, who
became Queen Elizabeth and
then the Queen Mother, steps
out with the Lord Mayor on
Processional Way in 1929
during a visit to Nottingham.
The Duke of York, later King
George VI, follows with the
Lady Mayoress.*

*The Duke and Duchess
of York at Harlow Wood
Hospital in 1929.*

King George VI and Queen Elizabeth are welcomed by the Lord Mayor of Nottingham on their arrival at the Council House for a six-hour visit in March 1943.

Princess Elizabeth, leaving Worksop Town Hall, in 1949, with Prince Philip, four years before her Coronation as Queen.

*Prince Charles,
suitably dressed,
leaves the cage at
the pithead at
Welbeck Colliery
during a visit in
1968.*

*The Queen unveils a commemorative
plaque at Worksop's Civic Buildings
with Bassetlaw Council chairman,
Councillor Terry Nicholson on the left.*

*Happier days –
Prince Charles
and Princess
Diana on a visit
to Nottingham in
March 1985.*

Princess Anne chats to Sarah Frymann of Carlton-le-Willows School and a teacher, Martin Roscoe, holding his baby daughter Hannah. Second left is Mrs B.Thorpe, area representative of the Save the Children Fund.

The Queen talks to schoolchildren on her arrival at Newark Railway Station in April 1984.

In the front line – youngsters of the Bowbridge Infants School, Newark, greet the Queen during her visit to Nottinghamshire.

Happy crowds lining the streets of Worksop for a glimpse of the Queen during her visit in June 1981.

Prince Charles walks through the grounds of Portland Training College, near Mansfield, with college principal Ken Gill during a visit to Nottinghamshire, in March 1985. Princess Diana sees the funny side of the conversation.

Smiling faces for Princess Diana on a walkabout in Old Market Square, Nottingham, in March 1985.

Prince Charles and Princess Diana thrill the crowds at Bestwood Lodge in March 1985.

Children from Saville House School, Mansfield Woodhouse, await the arrival of Prince Charles and Princess Diana during the 1985 visit.

Princess Anne gets the warmest of greetings in Arnold during a visit in November 1985.

Prince Charles congratulates fire crew on their skills demonstration at Bestwood in 1985.

Transport in Nottinghamshire

All set for the Clipstone motor trials shortly before World War One.

Ready for a trip out in the fresh air in Nottinghamshire but not at breakneck speed because a notice on the side of this charabanc says 'speed 12mph'. The picture is undated.

The birthplace of the Midland Railway, the Sun Inn at Eastwood, in September 1928. It was here that a group of Erewash coalowners decided to open the new railway, fearing that if George Stephenson continued to deliver coal from Leicestershire at less than 10s a ton on his new Leicester and Swannington line, Nottinghamshire coal would become uneconomic.

Not on service but still going strong in September 1954, this Barton bus, on the road from Beeston, was en route to the commercial motor show at Earls Court, London. The driver was C.R.Atkinson, accompanied by Mrs Atkinson.

Commercial and pleasure craft at the lock on the Trent at Stoke Bardolph in August 1937.

The first aircraft and crew of the Missionary Aviation Fellowship at Tollerton Airport in September 1947, during a tour of the country before setting off for a pathfinding mission to Central Africa. The aircraft is a twin-engined Miles Gemini, the Mildmay Pathfinder. The pilot, John Stuart Hemmings, of Nottingham, is second from the left, with navigator T.Banham, of Lowdham on his left.

The first five United States Air Force Dakota planes to be repaired by Field Aircraft Services at Tollerton, under a two million dollar contract, are pictured in Number One hangar workshop in January 1953.

Roy Cocking takes his friend Beryl for a leisurely drive by pony and trap on Musters Road, West Bridgford in September 1951.

The scene at Holme Lock, near Holme Pierrepont, in August 1957. The bathers, top left, were obviously preparing to take their lives in their hands by swimming in the Trent.

A barge carrying petrol to Nottingham cruises past the new power station at Staythorpe in August 1956.

The passage of the barge disturbs the tranquillity of the Trent at Hoveringham in August 1954.

This train of tankers from Ellesmere Port, Cheshire, to Colwick was solidly stuck in the snow, in February 1958, on the main Derby-Nottingham (Eastern) line at Nuthall Junction. Troops from Chilwell Depot were called in to help workmen dig the train out.

Maid Marian, *a Foster steam engine owned by Jess Swingler of West Bridgford is made ready for the road in October 1973, for a journey to Loughborough for a Main Line Trust exhibition. It was used to drive a showground organ.*

This March 1933 picture of the high level crossing over Nottingham Road on the approach to Toton accompanied a report in the Evening Post *on a proposal to replace it with a bridge. In its early years, the GNR called Toton the 'slaughter house of the Midland Railway' because of its poor safety record.*

On The Buses *actor Bob Grant and his wife Kim on an old Barton bus with the Tozer Babes in July 1983, before parading through Nottingham to their wedding celebrations.*

Four £1,000 winners in Broxtowe Borough Council's lottery were given a special trip in a vintage bus owned by Barton Transport of Beeston to receive their prizes in Old Market Square, Nottingham. The bus was driven by Barton employee Frank Garnham, left, of Chilwell, who was the first to receive the top award. With him are Rickki Pitman of Long Eaton, then the latest winner and former winners Mrs Jyllian Varney, of Chilwell and Jim Dobbs of Stapleford.

Pupils and staff of Foxwood School, Bramcote, take a ride back in time on the Barton charabanc which was used to launch its services after the company was established in 1908.

It looks like a scene in Singapore but this rickshaw ride was in Mansfield in 1978. Fruiterer Hampton Flint did his own Chinese take-away when he carried off pretty Yuk Kwai Liu, wife of restaurant-owner David Liu in a rickshaw on display outside Mr Flint's new shop.

A line-up of traction engines, possibly at Rempstone, in July 1974.

Steam enthusiast Philip Cundy and his bride Heather Sheppard, outside St Michael and All Saints Church, Stanton-by-Dale, after their wedding in 1982. The bride was saluted by three steamrollers blowing their whistles.

Big is beautiful but so is small. Demonstrating this are steam enthusiasts Barry Johnson and Brian Redfern. Barry, from Kegworth is driving a full-sized steamroller and Brian, of Burton upon Trent, is on a 4in to 1ft model. They were at the Bilborough Steam Rally in Wollaton Park.

Cyril Rose of Radcliffe-on-Trent, compares his half-size showman's traction engine with the real thing at Kegworth carnival in July 1976.

Stilt cyclist Ray King passes a Foden steam lorry at Kegworth Carnival in July 1986.

What a gorgeous sight – and the 1926 showman's engine is not bad-looking either! Helping out at the Rempstone Steam and Country Show in July 1984 are, left to right, Sally Burford, Pat Matthews, Helen Duggleby and Mary Morley.

The bells ring for a happy send-off for newly-weds Alan Campbell and Susan Attewell, in April 1977, on a double-decker bus as they leave Shakespeare Street Register Office, Nottingham. Alan and Susan both worked for Trent Motor Traction company, Alan as a mechanic and Susan as a cleaner.

Religious Figures and Churches

NOTTINGHAMSHIRE is the envy of the world for the quality and variety of its churches, ranging from the majestic Southwell Minster and Pugin-designed St Barnabus Roman Catholic Cathedral in Nottingham to Littleborough's tiny Norman church. In fact, the history of Christianity can be traced through visiting them. No one knows why so many religious leaders have hailed from, or had strong connections with Nottinghamshire but county folk have a reputation for independence of thought and this is no doubt one of the factors. The Pilgrim Father movement was started in the late sixteenth century in Babworth and Scrooby by William Brewster and William Bradford. Brewster's home became the meeting place but members of the first Separatist church were hounded by the authorities and after periods of having to lie low and exile in Holland, the two Nottinghamshire men sailed on the Mayflower with their followers to New England, USA, in 1620. George Fox, founder in the seventeenth century of the Quakers, originally based in the Mansfield area, spent eight terms in Nottingham Prison for his beliefs. There would be no Southwell Minster today but for another Nottinghamshire man, Edward Cludd, who as a county representative of the 'bare-bones parliament' of 1653, persuaded Oliver Cromwell not to knock it down.

The Holy Club, formed in 1729 by brothers John and Charles Wesley of Epworth, led to the development of Methodism and Sneinton's William Booth, a Methodist preacher at 17, founded the Salvation Army in Nottingham in 1878.

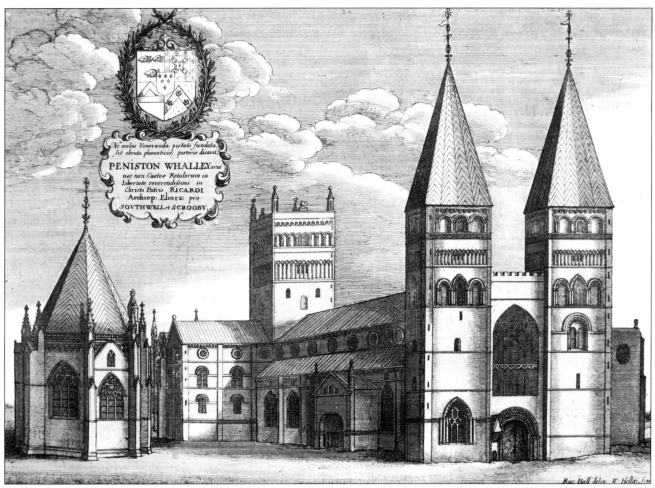

Southwell Minster, as it was drawn in 1677 by W.Hollar.

Bishop's Manor, Southwell.

Choirboys' surplices make a fluttering ribbon of white as 300 choristers walk in procession into Southwell Minster, ancient mother church of the diocese, at the 11th festival of choirs in July 1958.

The picturesque parish church at Oxton, bathed in spring sunshine in March 1968.

Norwell Church.

Newark Church, beautifully set in the centre of the town.

A cycling shepherd and his dog guide their flock past Laxton Church in October 1954.

Edwinstowe Church, where Robin Hood is said to have married Maid Marian.

The attractive and compact Langar Church.

With its octagonal lantern tower and a spire which is also octagonal, the church of St Mary at Keyworth is one of the most unusual churches in the country. This picture was taken in August 1985.

The old Bilsthorpe Church, which could accommodate only 85 people, including the choir.

An idyllic view of Averham Parish Church.

The church of St Edmunds, Mansfield Woodhouse, floodlit to mark its 650th anniversary, in September 1953.

The Parish Church of St Wilfrid's, Kirkby-in-Ashfield, which was listed as a building of special architectural or historic interest in January 1950.

Ratcliffe-on-Soar Church, surrounded by water in the floods of 1929.

Bell-ringers at Radcliffe-on-Trent Parish Church in about 1946.

*Radcliffe-on-Trent
Parish Church.*

*Annesley Church, which was
demolished in January 1907.*

All Saints Church, Annesley, which was abandoned when a new church was built a mile away to service the mining community. This picture was taken in June 1953.

Stoke Bardolph Church, showing the new chancel and vestry in June 1913.

The demolition of a number of old cottages opened up this 'new' view of Arnold Parish Church in October 1959.

St Mary's Church, Plumtree.

Fishpool Ebenezer Methodist Chapel, which had not been used for services for six years when this picture was taken in April 1955, was creating a problem for Mansfield Central Circuit Methodists because without a Home Office permit the building could be used for nothing but religious purposes because there was a grave beneath the central aisle.

A service goes on inside the bomb-damaged St Christopher's Church, Colwick, in 1941.

A lone soldier gets a fine view of Clumber Park Church in November 1962.

The impressive East Markham Church.

An old picture of the head of a Saxon Cross at Shelford Church.

Linby's ancient parish church, with its new clock, in June 1947. A legacy from a former rector enabled the church to buy the clock.

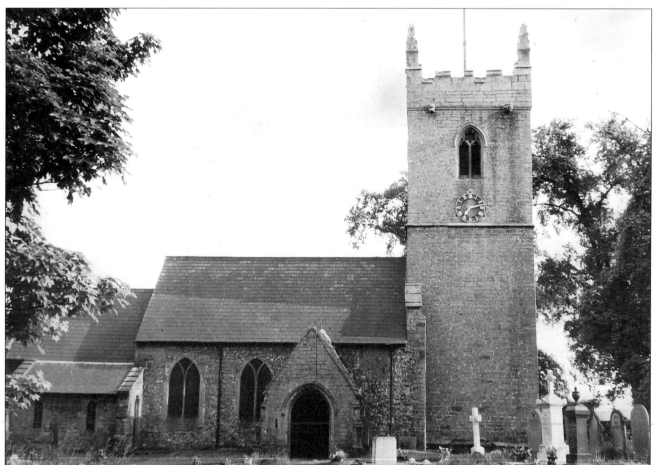

To many people the name Ollerton means busy crossroads and a mining community but the old part of the village, with its fine church, has a typically English rural aspect. This picture was taken in October 1972.

Bell-ringers Mick Exton and Miss Mary Gayden examine two new bells at Whatton Parish Church before they were hoisted into the belfry.

*Lambley Church makes a pleasing
background as the aptly-named local baker
S.M.Baker sets out on his rounds in July
1964.*

*Work in progress in 1960
on the tower of the
thirteenth-century church
of St Peter, Tollerton.*

The parish chest at Screveton, which is 6ft 9in long by 18 inches.

Ascension Day got off to an early start in Ruddington in May 1973, when members of the parish church choir and the Vicar, the Revd Clive Shrimpton, took part in a service on the church roof.

The distribution of bread, under the Thompsons Charity at St Peter's Church, Nottingham, in 1905.

The end of the line for St Thomas' Church, Park Row, Nottingham.

Jack Cook mows a grass verge in the grounds of Laxton's ancient church in May 1968.

St Mary's Church, Wollaton Park, architect T.Cecil Howitt.

Woodborough Church, decorated with flowers to celebrate its 600th birthday in July 1956.

Schools in Nottinghamshire

St John's Church Schools, Mansfield, at around the turn of the century.

The Lower Remove at Musters Road Infants School, West Bridgford, in 1941.

Pupils of Greasley Beauvale Infants School enjoy a taste of history in September 1985. The cake, in the shape of a book, was made to celebrate the centenary of the birth of D.H.Lawrence, a former pupil at the school.

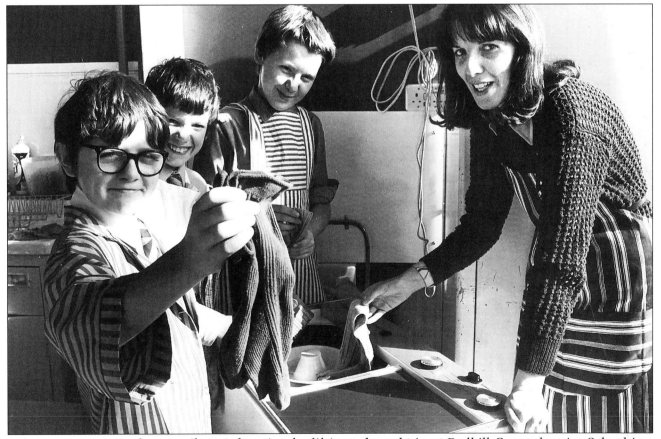

A new way to introduce pupils to 'education for life' was brought in at Redhill Comprehensive School in October 1977, with girls equally at home learning the skills of woodwork and metalwork as the boys were doing housecraft and home economics. Here, teacher Mrs Margaret Wilson shows boys how to use a twin-tub washing machine. Nigel Matthews brought along a pair of socks to launder.

Pupils of Woodthorpe County Infants School cross Arnold Vale Road, year unknown.

School meals supervisor Mrs Florence Rick is surrounded by children at Burford Primary School, Arnold, in July 1976. The occasion was her retirement after seven years and the children presented her with a bouquet and a vase. In the background are the headmaster Mr G.Mills and the school cook Mrs E.Edgson.

Mothers campaigning for a children's crossing warden form a human barrier across Portland Road, Hucknall, in January 1971, while pupils of Butler's Hill Infants School cross over. They later sent a petition to the Chief Constable.

This school, Spring Street Infants, Hucknall, closed in 1976 and became a new youth and community centre four years later. The building was then more than 100 years old.

Some of the children about to start school after Easter, 1970, get a taste of life at Carnarvon County Primary School, Bingham. They are, from the left, Joanna Hodson, Jane Evans, Jeremy Hall, Paula Bowden and Penny Thomas.

This electric pop-folk group from Keyworth Junior School, aged between nine and 11, tune up for auditions for Thames Television's Fanfare for Young Musicians in June 1982.

Pupils of Ruddington school line up to say farewell to Lollipop Lady Mrs Alice Adams on her retirement in March 1978.

Industry in Nottinghamshire

BRITAIN is an island built on coal and Nottinghamshire is a county whose prosperity was linked with it closely for many, despite a wide diversity of other industries ranging from hosiery, lace-making, telecommunications, textiles and shoes to gypsum, tobacco, bicycle production, brewing and pharmaceuticals. (Several of which are featured in *Images of Nottingham*, in this series.)

Sadly, because local mining families are the salt of the earth, there are now less than a handful of collieries in production in the county.

Yet as recently as October 1992, 200,000 people, including many from Nottinghamshire, marched through London to protest at a Government plan to close 31 pits with the loss of 30,000 jobs, leading to Michael Heseltine, then President of the Board of Trade, being forced to back down to avert a Government defeat in the Commons.

Coal was important to Nottinghamshire for many centuries. Eleanor, the wife of Henry 111, is said to have left Nottingham Castle because of the smell of sea coal in 1257. And in 1303 there was a major public protest over the 'obnoxious fuel'.

Many Nottinghamshire families can remember the 1926 pit strike. By the end of October that year, more than 200,000 miners had been starved back to work. The Nottingham mining MP George Spencer, meanwhile, was in dispute with the Miners' Federation over the creation of a breakaway 'non-political union'.

The NUM came into being on 1 January 1945. 1 January 1947, vesting day for the industry, marked the birth of the National Coal Board. By the following year, the average wage in the industry had risen to £7 17s a week.

A low for mining families came in January 1972, when more than a quarter of a million miners were on strike and every pit in Britain was at a standstill.

On 8 February, the Government imposed a three-day week on all industrial production and a 15 per cent cut in domestic consumption.

The Government capitulated and the miners won wage increases of £5 a week for surface workers, £6 for underground workers and £4.50 for face workers, plus fringe benefits.

The NUM called another pit strike for 10 February 1974, but 72 hours before it was due to start, Prime Minister Edward Heath called a General Election to try to defeat the militants. He failed, Labour being returned with a four-seat majority.

Within two days the board had given in to most of the NUM's demands and on 11 March the strike ended.

A revised Plan For Coal envisaged an output of 135 million tons in 1985, rising to 170 million tons in 2000. It proved wildly optimistic.

By October 1977, the NUM executive had approved a productivity deal with the Coal Board.

A miners' ballot turned it down but some areas, mainly in the East Midlands, made it clear they would go it alone by agreeing local incentive deals in defiance of the national ballot.

Even the forceful, emerging Arthur Scargill could not stop this and in less than two years every NUM area had made a productivity deal with the NCB.

The worst recession since the 1930s, which started in the early 1980s, hit the mining industry very badly, speeding up the closure of pit after pit.

Scargill was elected NUM President in December 1981, with 70.3 per cent of the vote. Yet moderation still ruled in the union as a whole. The 358-day long miners' strike of 1984-85, which escalated from local strikes in militant areas, led to the arrest of 9,000 miners and to the formation of a breakaway, moderate union in Notts, the Union of Democratic Mineworkers.

The strike ended on 5 March 1985, two days after the NUM decided by a narrow vote to call it off with no agreement.

It took great courage for the moderate miners of Nottinghamshire to stand up to the mass picketing and violence of such a long, bitter strike.

Without taking sides, it was a great shame that the rift between the moderates and militants – sometimes within the same families – developed as it did among 'brothers' in the toughest of industries.

Moderate Nottinghamshire miners make it clear, at a demonstration at Berry Hill in May 1984, that their 'no ballot, no strike' edict stands, despite the hotting up of the miners' strike in other areas.

An NUM picket lays the law down to a police officer in Nottinghamshire during the 1984-85 miners' strike.

The true character of the Nottinghamshire miner, rugged, tough but open, fair and friendly is reflected in Jack Beaston's face.

Miners on the march in the centre of Nottingham in April 1984.

Police out in force at Harworth Colliery, North Nottinghamshire, where miners decided in March 1984, not to cross the picket lines.

'Miners strike now', urge posters as this group make their point near Notts NUM headquarters at Berry Hill, while a short distance away, a large demonstration of moderates was urging the opposite view, 'no ballot, no strike' in May 1984. A stormy four and a half hour meeting of local NUM delegates there turned down, by more than 2-1, a top-level recommendation that miners should not cross picket lines and should form their own.

Pickets at the NCB's Bestwood Central Workshops, in Bestwood Village during the 1972 strike.

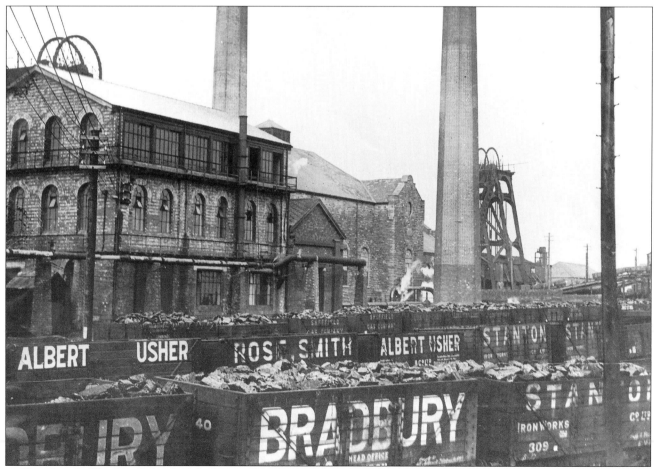

Pleasley Colliery as it looked in November 1926, as coal got on the move again after the General Strike.

Cinderhill Colliery sidings in December 1946.

Annesley Colliery – date unknown.

Linby Colliery, where some miners were on strike in 1953.

This picture, taken in Bestwood in September 1949, with the colliery in the background, will bring back a few memories.

The Bishop of Southwell (third, left), arriving to visit the coal face at Bestwood Colliery in October 1949. He is accompanied by the Revd G.Spittles (on his left), Rural Dean of Bulwell, and the Revd J.S.Lemon, Vicar of Stapleford and formerly Rector of Bestwood; Norman Siddall, agent; and Mr L.R.Boyfield, the colliery manager.

A typical Notts colliery village, Bestwood again, pictured in 1946.

The Lancaster Drift, Bestwood, which opened in May 1946, two years before this photograph was taken.

Hugh Gaitskell, Leader of the Opposition, left, on a visit to Calverton Colliery in June 1957, when he crawled 30 yards down a 3ft 6in seam to see a machine cutting and loading coal. With him is Mr N.R.Smith, area general manager.

Summit Colliery, Kirkby-in-Ashfield, in 1966.

Workmen drilling for a proposed new shaft at Hucknall Colliery in December 1957.

Another view of Annesley Colliery.

A previously unpublished picture of Thoresby Colliery, taken in January 1951.

If anyone asked for Mr Cubbin at Harworth Colliery in October 1964, when this picture was taken, he would have got at least eight replies, for Jack Cubbin had his seven sons working with him there. Back row, (left to right) are Jack, Cyril, Ernest and Frank. Front row: Owen, Terry, Dawson and Jackie.

These two winding structures at Clipstone Colliery were among the tallest, at 214ft, in the country when this picture was taken in January 1986.

Blidworth Colliery, year unknown.

All roads – or is it just a concrete path – lead to Ollerton Colliery.

The coke plant at Ollerton in October 1966.

A demonstration urging the development of Newstead Colliery in October 1970.

Dignatories from Nottinghamshire's county, borough and district councils, with company executives, on a visit to British Gypsum at East Leake in May 1990.

Originally the sails of North Leverton windmill brushed the ground but by the time this picture was taken in the 1960s, they had been fitted with patent flaps which were much easier to work as the grain was ground.

One of the original Rolls-Royce test pilots who flew the 'Flying Bedstead', forerunner of all vertical lift-off aircraft, holds up a model of the machine in July 1993, at the 40th anniversary celebrations at Hucknall to mark the company's work in this sphere. An RAF Harrier Jump-jet, a descendant of the Bedstead, flew in to take part in the celebrations.

GPT's System X development director at Beeston, Jack Dawson, holds up a £1 billion British Telecom contract, in September 1990, which meant that the country's telephone exchanges were halfway to being completely digitalised. It was the biggest single order the company had ever won.

A quartet with 132 years service between them say farewell to Plessey Telecommunications on their retirement in June 1978. With them are two members of the company's Pensions and Welfare Department, Mrs Kathy Hughes, left, and Mrs Doris Taylor, right, the manager. The quartet are, left to right, Eric Kingsland, Mrs Fay Warriner, Ron Gunson and Frederick Penniston.

Albert Cano, then 16, from Stapleford, tries out wiring work and printed circuit board assembly in the training centre at Plessey during a visit to the Beeston factory in March 1979. With him are John Scott, left, Foxwood's deputy headteacher and Frank Philipson, Plessey's apprentice training manager.

Drilling for oil in Eakring in 1952.

Floods in Nottinghamshire

Floods in Loughborough Road, West Bridgford, in 1946.

The water in this section of Bridgford Road, West Bridgford, near the park, was 5ft deep in parts in the floods of 1946.

These cars just managed to keep going in flood-hit Musters Road, West Bridgford. Picture: J.D.Whitworth.

Deliveries of the Evening News *beat the floods in the Nottingham area in March 1947.*

People are ferried across Loughborough Road, West Bridgford, in the floods of 1947.

Men of the Royal Engineers ferry West Bridgford people under the LMS bridge on Bridgford Road during the great floods of 1947.

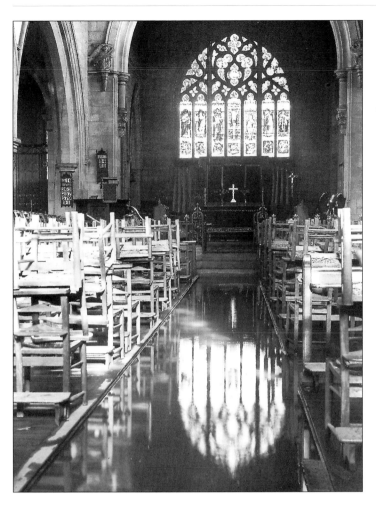

It looks bad enough as it is but the flood water in St Giles Church, West Bridgford, had subsided considerably when this picture was taken in March 1947.

Mrs Doris Green still manages a smile as she puts a sandbag on the doorstep of her bungalow in Leeway Road, Southwell, in December 1965.

Anthony Potts exercising Copes Cross for Mr P.Green on the flooded banks of the River Trent at Gunthorpe in December 1965.

Shoppers marooned at the GEM Supercentre (now Asda), West Bridgford, are ferried to dry ground by staff after a freak storm brought flooding in August 1967.

The Unicorn Hotel, Gunthorpe, is cut off by flood water in December 1960.

'Bingham-on-Sea' in 1967. A fire appliance at work on the corner of Church Street, Bingham, after a heavy storm flooded the town.

It's a proper knees-up in the centre of Bingham during the 1967 floods.

The Historic Town of Newark

BY THE time Charles I started the Civil War in August 1642, when he raised the Royal Standard on Castle Hill, Nottingham, he had already secured the strategic town of Newark, whose Castle fortress and position on the River Trent gave it great military importance.

He did not get much support in Nottingham but a speech to the knights, gentlemen and freeholders of Newark on 12 July that year had won them over, not least because he had often visited the town.

Parliamentary forces came close to capturing Newark during a siege the following February and a year later only a charge from Prince Rupert's forces down Beacon Hill saved it after it was surrounded by a force of 8,500 men.

In October 1645, Charles I dismissed Prince Rupert from Generalship after a quarrel in the Governor's House in Newark and left the town in a considerable hurry on 3 November as Parliament, backed by a strong Scottish army, tried again, unsuccessfully, to take it.

On 6 May, Charles, after giving himself up to the Scots, ordered the Governor of Newark to surrender the town. He had returned to Newark the previous day.

After the Newark garrison marched out, unbowed, on 9 May the Castle was reduced to ruins.

The King was executed on 30 January 1649, and a period of religious freedom under Oliver Cromwell followed until his death in 1658.

The Stuart monarchy was restored in 1660 and 30 years of religious persecution followed as the Law set out to destroy the spirit of Independency.

This had considerable implications in Newark, as elsewhere. Even before the Act of Uniformity came in, the Revd John James, a lecturer, was thrown into jail for refusing to give up preaching.

Later, five aldermen of Newark were sacked from their posts because they would not take Communion under Anglican rites.

In November 1659 Quakers at a meeting in Newark were stoned and severely beaten while William Dewsbury was preaching.

In February 1687, James II ordered the removal of the Mayor of Newark and five aldermen.

The old Parliament House, Newark, which became the Arcade.

Newark Market Place in 1844.

Newark's Kirk Gate in 1836.

Newark, looking along Kirk Gate towards the church.

Newark Market Place has not changed all that much since this picture was taken in August 1958.

A barge makes its way upstream, in September 1965, towards Newark's ruined Castle.

Mrs Daisy Wilcox, chairman of Newark District Council, and the Bishop of Southwell, the Right Revd Denis Wakeling, cut turfs from the site of the new St Leonard's Church, Lincoln Road, Newark, in October 1977. The church was to replace the one in Northgate.

Left: These girls are taking extra care as they walk across Newark's cobbled Market Square in November 1969, for many women had stumbled on the uneven surface. The cobbles had been cleaned and relaid to preserve the market's old world appearance.

Right: Beamond Cross, Newark, which has stood at the junction of the Great North Road and the Fosse Way since 1310, pictured in May 1958. The origin and reason for the cross are not known. Popular theory has it that it is one of a series of Queen Eleanor crosses marking the resting places on her funeral procession to Westminster.

Freddie Trueman, the legendary England fast bowler, in Newark in April 1973, on a sponsored horse ride for charity from York to London, dressed as the highwayman Dick Turpin. Trueman, raising money for the Variety Club of Great Britain, is held up himself by the Mayoress of Newark, Mrs A.G.Hine, but only to persuade him to autograph a cricket ball bought by the Mayor of Newark, Councillor A.G.Hine, which was auctioned for the fund.

Fiery Fred Trueman rides around Newark Market Place during his stop-off in the town in 1973.

The Ancient Town of Mansfield

IN 1927 Mansfield had possibly the biggest double celebration in its long history, the 700th anniversary of the granting of the Market Charter by Henry III and 550th anniversary of the granting by Richard II of the July Fair.

The town goes back a long, long way. A flint axe-head dug up in Stockwell Gate showed that there were settlers there in the Neolithic Age and the Romans are known to have had a settlement there.

In Henry VIII's reign, the Manor of Mansfield, not for the first time, was granted as a reward for services to the State. It went this time to the Duke of Norfolk for his gallantry at Flodden Field. His brief connection is marked by two crosslets on the town's crest.

The Manor played a part in the formation of the Royal Forest of Sherwood. It was a favourite hunting ground for the Saxon Kings and the Plantaganets. This led to a area of land on Berry Hill being given the name King's Stand.

Mansfield was a stronghold of Presbyterianism in the seventeenth century and had large numbers of Quakers.

The town suffered badly in the plague in 1631.

One of its claims to fame is that a resident, Joseph Murray, invented the circular saw, trying it first on a carrot.

The Mansfield to Pinxton Railway opened in 1810. Trucks were drawn by bullocks and horses until midway through the nineteenth century when it was taken over by the Midlands County Railway Co., who turned it from a tramway into a proper railway.

The Market Place assumed its new shape in 1840, in time for the July Fair. The Town Hall was built in 1836. The gas works were completed in 1824 at a cost of £5,000.

In 1867 a cottage hospital was opened, followed by the official opening in 1889 of the hospital in West Hill Drive to commemorate Queen Victoria's Golden Jubilee.

Mansfield Police Court was built in 1973 in Commercial

Street after being at the Town Hall since 1836.

The town has always had a variety of industries. It became one of the centres of the hand-knitted worsted hose industry from the sixteenth century because wool from the Sherwood Forest sheep produced a yarn of unrivalled quality.

It survived as a force for 40 years after William Lee's invention of the stocking frame in 1589. As far back as 1800 the town had up to 700 hand-frames.

But its prosperity was founded on the wealth of coal under it. A publication on the Borough of Mansfield in 1927 said that pits inside a radius of eight miles from Mansfield Town Hall were producing 100,000 tons of coal a day.

Magnesium limestone from Mansfield was used in the building of the Houses of Parliament and in the Albert Memorial.

A brewery was established in the town in 1854 and a maltings was built many years before that.

From modest beginnings in 1890, the fancy tin box-making industry in the town became the finest in the land.

A water colour of old Mansfield, year unknown.

Lifeboat Saturday in Mansfield, in about 1900, was celebrated by a visit of this boat. Manned by the lifeboat crew, it was brought to give a demonstration on King's Mill Reservoir and other events were held during the day to raise funds for the lifeboat service. Standing in front of the boat is Jesse Moore, then headmaster of St John's Church of England School.

The opening of Mansfield gasometer in 1902.

The 40ft diameter waterwheel at Field Mill in 1910, which was demolished in 1925. It was situated on Nottingham Road on a site where the Imperial Laundry was later built.

Leeming Street, Mansfield, in July 1912.

The Swan Inn, Mansfield, c.1900, with a carriage coming in from Church Street.

The gates are opened and children run for the traditional distribution of hot cross buns at the Old Meeting House, Stockwell Gate, Mansfield.

Useful in a shower – this curiously-shaped hawthorn, known as Table Top Tree, was pictured beside the Nottingham-Mansfield road near Fountain Dale in November 1958.

This tank was presented to the town of Mansfield in 1919.

Eyes down for a lollipop stick race in Mansfield's Titchfield Park in May 1971.

The end for this old railway bridge over the A617 at Rainworth in December 1972.

An undated picture of J.Aldridge's ironmonger shop in Mansfield.

Nelson's guns which fired at the Battle of Trafalgar had their fittings moulded in Mansfield sand and this giant 'pile' of it was pictured in 1952, in the Berry Hill area. The red mineral has a moulding quality seldom found elsewhere in any quantity.

The Fair Town of Southwell

SOUTHWELL has always been special. The Manor was given by King Eadwug to Oskytel, Archbishop of York, in 956. A college of priests was established there a century later and from then on the Minster, the mother church of Nottinghamshire, was regarded as a sub-cathedral in the Archdiocese of York.

The collegiate foundation survived the Reformation but was abolished in 1841. The new Diocese of Southwell was formed in February 1884, when the Minster became its cathedral.

Burgage Manor in the town is where Lord Byron and his mother lived when he inherited Newstead Abbey, because they did not have the money to make it fit to live in.

Southwell marked its centenary in 1984 and the Queen presented the Royal Maundy money there as part of the celebrations.

King Charles I leaving the old courtyard of the Saracen's Head Inn, Southwell, in 1646.

An undated picture of the market place and Saracen's Head, Southwell, with the Assembly Rooms in the background.

Everything revolves around the Saracen's Head including this meeting of the hunt, year not known.

An old wedding custom, walking through a tree, at Southwell in 1922.

Sporting Nottinghamshire

We are the champions! Nottingham Forest fans salute their heroes from the terraces at Coventry after the Reds won the point that gave them the Division One title in April 1978.

A delighted fan hugs Kenny Burns after Forest's point at Coventry in April 1978 which meant they were Football League champions.

Forest skipper John McGovern receives the League championship trophy in May 1978.

Wing wizard John Robertson holds the European Cup aloft in 1979 after his team, Nottingham Forest, had beaten Malmö FF 1-0 in the Final thanks to a Trevor Francis header from Robertson's cross.

Tony Woodcock, left, and John Robertson celebrate their first European Cup Final win in 1979.

This was the scene that greeted the victorious Nottingham Forest team outside County Hall when they showed off the European Cup in May 1979.

Heady days at Notts County in the Tommy Lawton era. The great man is in the centre of the front row, of course, in this team picture in May 1949. Back row (left to right): Southwell, Howe, Brown, Gannon, Corkhill, Plumbley. Front row: Freeman, Sewell, Lawton, Marsh and Houghton.

Division One here we come! Notts County celebrate after winning a place in the top flight, before the Premier League was formed, in the Play-off Final at Wembley in 1991. Manager Neil Warnock is standing, left.

The faces say it all. Tommy Johnson and manager Neil Warnock in seventh heaven after their Wembley win which put the Magpies back into the First Division.

Mansfield Town players celebrate at Wembley after winning the Freight/Rover Trophy Final in May 1987.

Mike Graham and George Foster, right, are ecstatic after the final penalty save by Kevin Hitchcock gave Mansfield the Freight/Rover Trophy at Wembley in May 1987.

Sue Henson of Gedling blows up the judges' tower at Nottingham's Colwick Park Racecourse in July 1987. It was her prize in one of the more unusual Evening Post *competitions. The tower was erected in 1949 and was redundant because the judges moved to the new stand.*

The shell of Colwick Racecourse grandstand after a mystery blaze destroyed it in March 1986.

Firemen making sure the Colwick grandstand is safe after the fire.

Jockey Jonjo O'Neill, left, takes a close look at the plaque he unveiled in April 1987, after the reopening of the grandstand at Colwick Racecourse after a fire. Also in the picture are Lord Gainsborough, centre, chairman of the racecourse and David Henson, clerk of the course.

The Halam hurdle race at Southwell Racecourse in May 1958.

The test – jockeys and mounts thunder over the new Fibresand strip at Southwell Racecourse in August 1989.

Richard Cordon, then aged two, tries to spot his selection with grandad Douglas Cordon, of Bulwell, during a National Hunt meeting at Colwick Park in February 1988.

Mrs Midge Burridge, wife of owner James Burridge, unveils a plaque to open the new Centenary Stand at Colwick Park Racecourse in February 1992, to celebrate 100 years of racing there.

Chris Broad gives skipper Clive Rice a soaking but he wouldn't let go of the NatWest Bank Trophy which Nottinghamshire County Cricket Club won in 1987, along with the Britannic Assurance Championship. They were also Refuge Assurance Sunday League runners-up.

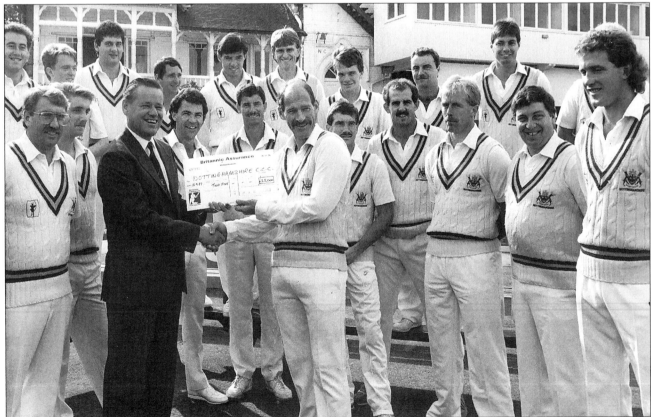

Michael Willett, chairman of Britannic Assurance, hands over a cheque for £25,000 to Nottinghamshire County Cricket Club captain Clive Rice, at Trent Bridge in September 1987, after they had won the County Championship.

Nottinghamshire County Cricket Club players arrive at County Hall in September 1987, for a civic reception to mark their remarkable double.

The man in white, world champion Aidan Trimble, is the athlete who established Nottingham as the karate centre of Europe. Here, with European champion Ken Johnson, he gives a lesson in the sport to pupils of East Bridgford Primary School in February 1984.

Prime Minister Edward Heath opens the National Water Sports Centre, Holme Pierrepont, near Nottingham, in July 1973.

Eight Nottinghamshire Young Conservative groups competed in the first-ever YC raft race at the National Water Sports Centre. Here, a happy Tricia Sutcliffe hangs on to the mast while fellow matelots Brian Irving, right, and Ian Domelow do the paddling. They were all from Beeston Young Conservatives.

An aerial view of the National Water Sports Centre.

British under-13
squad member
Aimi Yeatman
from Long Eaton
shows off her
water-skiing skills
at the 21st
birthday
celebrations of the
National Water
Sports Centre,
Holme Pierrepont
in May 1994.

A talented foursome of Nottingham Panthers'
players in 1948. They are, left to right, Walt
Black, Ken Westman, Ed Young (captain) and
Roger Goodman.

Maurice La Forge, a former Nottingham Panthers' player, with his bride, Miss Joyce E.Hayes, of Nottingham, after their wedding at St Barnabus Cathedral in February 1952.

Chick Zamick, Nottingham Panthers' new coach (standing, top right) in a tactical talk with his players when practice for the new season started in October 1955.

A look behind the scenes at Nottingham Ice Stadium before Panthers' game with Paisley Pirates in October 1956.

Chick Zamick, right, in a duel for the puck with Wembley Lions' defenceman Roy Shepherd.

Spectators at Nottingham Ice Stadium get a close-up of Eddy Plata (Panthers) and Gerry Corriveau (Paisley Pirates) as they race along the boards in February 1958.

Nottingham Panthers line up for the 1984-85 season. Back row (from left): Steve Salter, Mark Goldby, Nigel Rhodes, Layton Eratt, Jason Wright. Middle row: Gavin Fraser, Andy Linton, John Bremner, Ged Smith, Mike Urquhart (coach), Dwayne Keward, Phil Adams. Front row: Chris Keward, Jeff Andison, Gary Keward (manager), Frankie Killen. Russ Timmins missed the team photograph.

Nottingham Panthers' ice hockey stars share their Cup Final triumph with two fans who missed out on the big match. Twin brothers Brian and George Pierrepont, seated, centre, were injured in a road accident on their way to the Norwich Cup Final at Birmingham's NEC in which Panthers beat Fife Fliers. The Panthers took the Cup, together with signed photographs, to the twins' Bakersfield home. Team members are, from left, Jim Keyes, Terry Kurtenbach, coach Alex Dampier and Fred Perlini.

Jubilant Nottingham Panthers celebrate their biggest success for over 30 years after roaring into the Final of the Norwich Cup in November 1986. They went on to win it.

Two down, one to go. Nottingham Panthers' player-coach Terry Gudziunas cracks open a bottle full of cash for cancer research, watched by his teammates and Paul De'ath (extreme right), landlord of the Magpies public house, Meadow Lane. From the left are John Bremner, Gavin Fraser (partly hidden), Gudziunas, Gary Clarson, Dave Welch, Andy Linton and Kenny MacDonald. The picture was taken in October 1982.

Lawrence Jackson, director and general manager of Crosland Filters, Nottingham Panthers' team sponsors in September 1985, lines up with the team to launch a major new sponsorship deal.

Nottingham Panthers' players cheer themselves up in the dressing-room in April 1986, after a defeat by Murrayfield put them out of the British Championship.

Nottingham Panthers' fans camping out in February 1987 for a ticket for the British Championship Play-offs the following month.

After the coldest night in Nottingham for 23 years in January 1987, this Nottingham Panthers' quartet found a home from home in the snow. The ice hockey-playing Canadians, left to right, Terry Kurtenbach, coach Alex Dampier, Jimmy Keyes and Randall Weber were used to playing in sub-zero temperatures and made light of the Arctic conditions.

Nottingham Cougars' line-up in March 1988. Back row (left to right): Robin White, Nicky Balchin, Duncan King, Jim Roebuck, Matt Flint (assistant coach), Harry Todd (manager), Russ Timmins (coach), Trevor Pickering, Danny White, Simon Perkins, Stuart Parker. Front row: David Selby, Chris Wilson, Simon Hunt, Grant Budd, Gary Rippingale, Mark Roberts, Geoff Boulter.

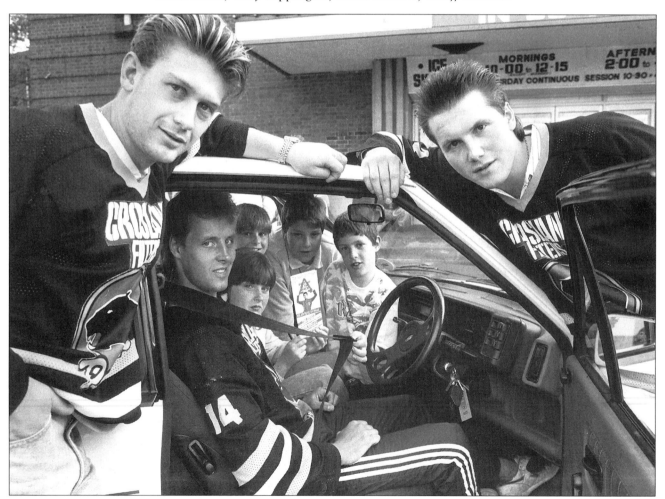

Nottingham Panthers are only too happy to belt up and lend their support to a road safety campaign. Members of the team were supporting the Kwik Fit Belt Up Campaign, in May 1989, in which local schools were encouraging people to wear seat-belts in both the front and rear of their cars. Players (from the left) John Hobson, Nigel Rhodes and James Elliott are seen with pupils from Beeston Rylands School.

Nottingham Panthers' stars at a presentation evening at the Commodore International in April 1989, after they had been crowned Heineken British Champions. Coach of the Year Alex Dampier, who turned his back on Peterborough to stay with Panthers, got a standing ovation. Pictured with their awards and the championship trophy are: Back row (left to right): Doc Durdle, Simon Perkins and Alex Dampier. Middle row: Paul Adey and Randall Weber. Front row: David Graham, Terry Kurtenbach and Mark Steeples.

They might look an old, unfit lot but these would-be hockey players helped to raise £2,000 for the Muscular Dystrophy charity in May 1989. These dads, and one or two guests, played their under-13 sons from the Nottingham Tigers at the Ice Stadium. The dads lost 7-2.

Crunch! Hucknall Town defender Ian Hammond is sandwiched between Bulwell United forwards Mark Beldham, left, and Kuki Morley as keeper Wayne Lear punches clear, in a pre-season game in August 1990.

Hucknall Town, who beat Grantham Town 2-1 in an FA Cup qualifying round match in September 1992. Back row (left to right): M.Vinter, C.Jones, D.Wainwright, L.Farmery, S.Borucki, C.Burton, P.Tomlinson, R.Harris, W.Scott, T.Preece. Front row: L.Holmes, J.Chamberlain, T.Smith, M.Smoczyk, P.Towle and J.Simpson.

Around and About Nottinghamshire

This old cottage at Calverton, where the Revd William Lee, in 1589, invented the stocking frame which revolutionised the hosiery industry, was renovated in 1971 as a local history museum.

This late eighteenth-century stocking frame was found in the loft of an old farm by pupils of Huthwaite Secondary School, Sutton-in-Ashfield, in 1968.

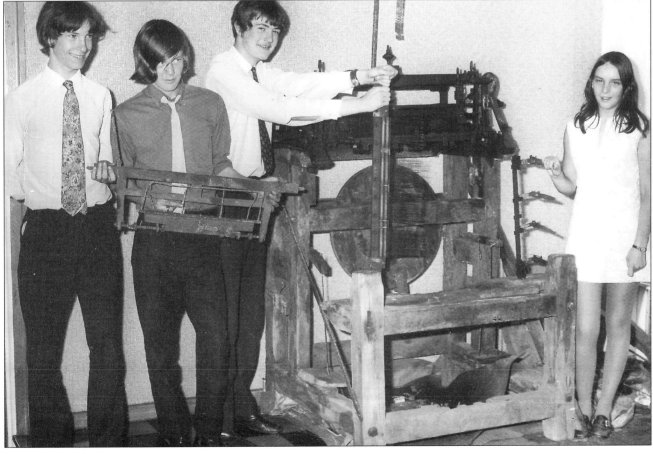

A drawing of a stocking frame similar to William Lee's.

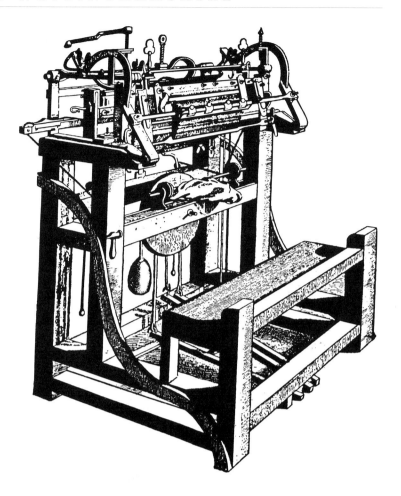

One of two sets of governors which controlled the beam engines built by James Watt and Co in 1884 at Papplewick pumping station.

This stone was erected in memory of 17-year-old Elizabeth Sheppard of Papplewick, who was murdered when passing the spot, not far from her home, by Charles Rotheram in 1817.

The little-known memorial at Papplewick to Thomas Gray, the poet.

Market Place, Retford in 1907.

Hucknall Excelsior Prize Band, c.1918.

Truman's Lodge, leading to Clumber Lane, one of the entrances to Clumber Park, which was opened to the public after its de-requisitioning by the Army in 1955.

The filter beds at Stoke Bardolph pictured in September 1936.

The ballroom at Bestwood Lodge in August 1926.

The seals of the Kings of Arms are on the bottom of this scroll which proclaims the granting of arms to Arnold Urban Council in April 1948.

The new fire station in Arnold in October 1935. The fire engine was leaving on its first call, but only for demonstration purposes.

When horse power was exactly that. A scene at Newton in September 1936.

The crowds get a close-up of aircraft at a show at Hucknall Aerodrome in May 1937.

Sweeping clean at Cotgrave shopping centre in May 1974.

The ancient village cross at Colston Bassett, completely restored in 1942.

Those were the days – or were they? An idyllic scene in Screveten in 1929.

A street scene in Worksop in 1907.

Competitors in a driving class assemble before their six-mile marathon at Thoresby Hall in May 1975.

The famous forge at Plumtree is in use again, in April 1947, proving, says the original caption, that despite mechanical innovations the countryman still has faith in his horses. Here, Albert Hogg is hard at work shoeing a horse. The forge was one of only two in the country built to a unique design.

An unusual sight in Plumtree as steamroller driver G.R.Stevenson enlists the help of Albert Hogg, the village blacksmith, in February 1951.

Festivity in Bingham's 'new' market place to celebrate its reopening for trading in July 1960.

East Bridgford's old windmill in March 1964, when it was 129 years old.

The interior of the old East Bridgford mill in 1965 after it was transformed into a luxury home.

This picture is old, but not as old as it looks! The occasion was a fancy dress party in Rufford in 1923.

The Round House on the fringe of Colwick Racecourse in February 1956. It was demolished in 1967.

A rich harvest of daffodils in Woodborough in April 1954.

This group of youngsters get their skates on the Grantham Canal at the side of Radcliffe Road, West Bridgford, in December 1950.

Members of Nottingham Ice Speed Club help two girls on the frozen Grantham Canal at West Bridgford in February 1952.

Miners pulling flax by hand at Newstead Grange Farm, Linby, in July 1953, after rain had flattened the crop, making the use of machinery impossible.

This grim-looking house is where the Pilgrim Fathers started. Scrooby Manor, Scrooby, was where William Brewster founded his pilgrim church.

The Revd F.J.Legge, Rector of East Leake, with some of the younger riders who took part in a service on Horseman's Sunday, in 1972.

Negotiating the stepping stones at East Leake in July 1963.

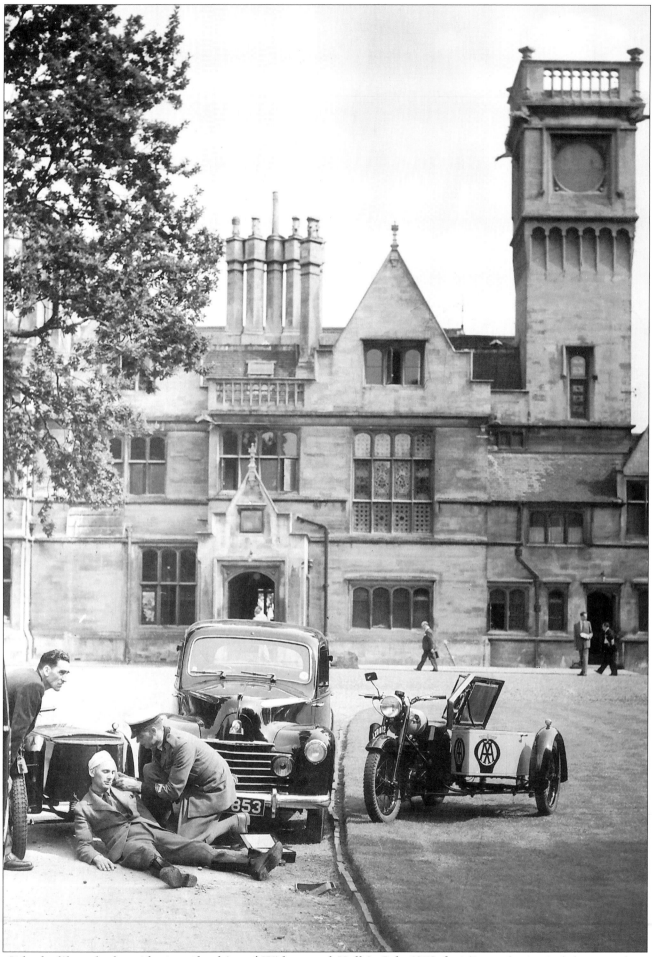

It looks like a bad accident on the drive of Widmerpool Hall in July 1952, but it was just a training exercise.

The scene in Main Street, Ruddington, in April 1966.

Ice frolics on the Grantham Canal in January 1954.

Who needs cars? The horse dominates in Southwell in 1972.

Rod Nixon, jack of all trades in pantomime, sorts out the cast of Aladdin and His Wonderful Lamp, *presented by staff and friends of Saxondale Hospital. Rod, a charge nurse, had been actor, director, producer, costume-maker and designer over a 12-year period.*

West Bridgford Urban Council at their diamond jubilee meeting in January 1955, at the Nottinghamshire County Cricket Club pavilion where the first meeting was held 60 years before.

Do you recognise it? Lady Bay Bridge, West Bridgford in 1937.

There is a real carnival spirit in this picture of the children's corner at West Bridgford Hall, for the town's Holidays-at-Home Week in August 1945.

Kingston Hall gardens in May 1950.

The Duke of Rutland's Hounds, in front of Langar Hall, in February 1935.

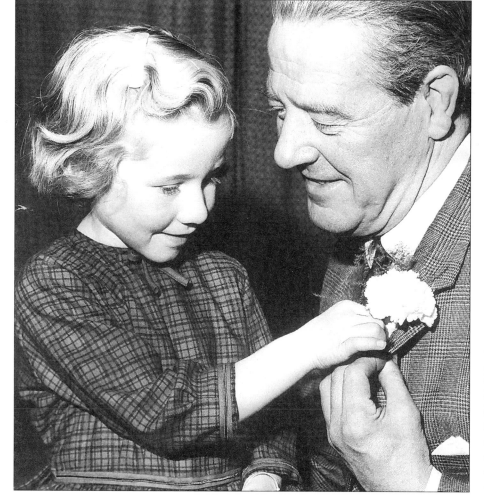

Philip Garston Jones, Jack Woolley in the radio serial The Archers, *receives a buttonhole from Christine Page, after he opened the Langar-cum-Barnstone Institute autumn fair at Barnstone in October 1966.*

The Battle of Britain was recalled by this display at Newton Aerodrome in September 1952.

Some things never change. The popularity of Gunthorpe Bridge has not waned since this picture was taken in June 1960.

IN
COMMEMERATION OF THE
ESTABLISHMENT OF THE
SHERWOOD COUNTRY PARK
AND THE PART PLAYED BY
C.C. MIRIAM BEARDSLEY
IN STIMULATING PUBLIC OPINION,
THESE TREES WERE PLANTED BY
THE EDWINSTOWE PARISH COUNCIL
1969.

David Greenslade, who played a part in the raising of a 45,000-name petition protesting at the use of part of Sherwood Forest by the Army, turfs in a stone, in 1969, commemorating the establishment of the Sherwood Country Park and the part played by county councillor Miriam Beardsley in 'stimulating interest' in the issue.

Mrs Mary Greig, of Rainworth, with her daughter Tammy, 17 months old in November 1972, when this picture was taken, and seven-year-old son Stephen, at a protest organised by local parents on Kirklington Road, Rainworth, after three children, including Mrs Greig's daughter Amanda, were killed near the spot in 14 months.

A scene at the Trent Boating Association River Trent rally at Colwick in June 1965.

This monument in Bunny Church was erected to the memory of Sir Thomas Parkyns, the Wrestling Baronet.
The picture was taken in July 1935.

Ordered charm on a sunny afternoon at Lowdham Mill in September 1954.

Cubs lead the clean-up in Tollerton in April 1974.

An aerial view of Rufford Abbey in 1949.

King Edward VII slept in this bed at Rufford Abbey. The picture was taken in January 1949.

Tom Fool of the Tollerton Plough Boys presents the collecting box at the close of their performance in the village.

Part of the main street at Woodborough as it was in June 1956.

Preparing the grounds at Papplewick Hall, ready for them opening to the public in June 1960.

This Wesleyan Sunday School parade in Arnold was c.1915. St Alban's Picturedrome is on the right.

The sun-dappled lake at Arnot Hill Park, Arnold, is just the spot for fishing in September 1961.

Front Street, Arnold, centre of a parking controversy in April 1968.

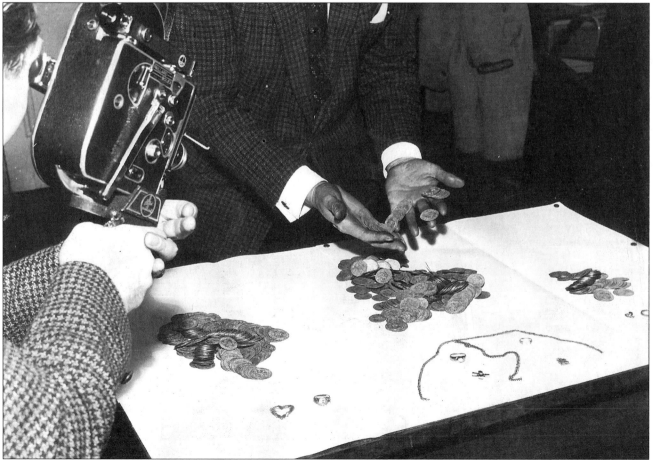

TV cameras focus on a collection of golden coins, a locket and chain and a brooch, found on a building site at Fishpool, near Newstead Abbey in December 1966.

David Walham, aged seven when this picture was taken, and Bernard Beeton, a lorry driver, who were to receive about £40,000 for their finds of rare gold medieval coins in the £250,000 Fishpool hoard.

The Fishpool haul of coins. What a find!

The unveiling of the Bonington tablet at Arnold Labour Party Club in October 1929.

Colwick Woods Park in October 1943.

Hucknall Parish Church in March 1967.

Woodborough, best-kept village in August 1966.

Bestwood Lodge, Arnold, as it was in 1938.

Marshall Nixon (with paper under his arm), engineer to the Trent River Board, conducts members of the board round the site of the new flood control sluices which were under construction at Colwick when members of the board paid a visit there in March 1954.

The girl with military bearing guarding the big gun in Retford's Cannon Square is model Beryl Sanderson, setting her sights on raising funds for a cancer detection charity. The cannon was captured in the Battle of Sebastopol in the siege of 1855.

Major-General C.L.Firbank inspecting Welbeck College Combined Cadet Force before a march past at which he took the salute at Welbeck College in June 1955.

Pre-Sandhurst training awaits these boys being shown round the grounds of Welbeck College by Mr L.C.Moss, head of the Department of Arts and Languages in September 1953.

Circus elephants take a dip in the dam next to what was in 1935, when this picture was taken, Tetley's latest Worksop pub, The Mill House.

*The Zachariah
Green monument,
erected in Hucknall
in 1898.*

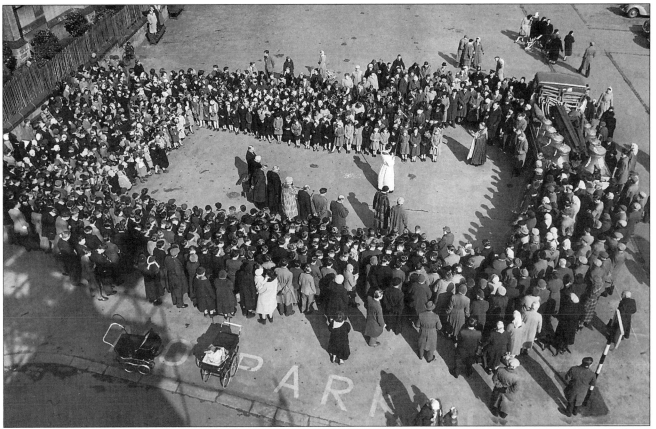

The scene in Hucknall Market Place in March 1958, when Canon K.G.Thompson, the vicar, blessed the new peal of bells for the parish church.

A fighter of 504 (County of Nottingham) Squadron in action during a display at Hucknall Aerodrome in May 1938.

This mobile crane ran out of control and crashed into number 79 Lowmoor Road, Kirkby-in Ashfield, in October 1970.

The 99-year-old railway viaduct across the River Maun and Quarry Lane, Mansfield, is blown up in June 1970.

The dead stump of a once great tree, the Greendale Oak in Sherwood Forest.

Children crossing the new by-pass at Balderton in August 1964. The Transport Minister Ernest Marples ruled out a footbridge over the southern end of by-pass because of the cost.

Subscribers

Age Concern, West Bridgford
Maureen Aitken
Harry Aldridge
Joe Frobisher Alltoft
John & Jan Anderson
Mrs Shirley Aplin
John & Allison Armstrong
John A Baker
Terence E Balchin
Kenneth Thomas Ball
Alan Bamford
John Barrowcliffe
Mr C A S Bell
Mrs Anne Benson
Eric J Berry
Mrs Joan Best
Patricia Bestwick
Susan I Bevan
Mrs Joan E Bexon
Ian Paul & Karen Biddulph
Jean Ann & Brian Biddulph
T W Birch
Paul A Bloomer
Mr & Mrs J Boaden
Audrey Booth
Mr & Mrs J G Booth
Alan Booton
Jean & John Boseley
P Bosworth
David A Breedon
R Brindley
Mrs J A Brinsley
John Brock
E Brown
Jenny & Richard Burnet
William Robert Francis Burton
G G Butler
Margaret Butlin
W H Campion
Barry Carnell
R M Carter
Alec Casterton
Tim Chamberlin
Dr M J Chappell
S P Cheeseman
Paul Michael Chettle
Bryce John Clare
Catherine R Clark
Peg & Tom Clark
Carole Clements
Martin H Clowes
Eric Cook
Peter F Cooke
Brian Cottingham
Mr & Mrs Cowdell
William Leslie & Doris Cramp
Stephen Cutts

John William & Maureen Ann Dack
J A Dale
Henry Victor Davies
Mr John Davies
Mrs Marion A Davis
Phyllis M Dawn
Derek Daykin
John Evatt Dexter
Eva Dickens
Dennis Disney
Morag Dolby
Mr & Mrs Donlan
Mr K Donlan
T G B Donlan
Barbara Dunleavy
Mrs K Eardley
Mrs Emily M Eaton
Jonathan M Eaton
Mrs J M Edwards
Mrs J M Edwards
M A Edwards
P G Edwards
Vera Irene Edwards
Mr & Mrs R N Epton
Mr Stuart Fenton & Mrs Pauline Fenton
K I Ferguson
Mr Trevor Fletcher
Graham Fowler
Frances Freeman
Mr & Mrs C A Frost
Mrs G E A Fyles
Mrs Doris Gamble
Mr Harold Francis Gascoyne
Mrs P Gilbert
Peter Gill
Richard J Gill
Clive Gilliatt
Tony & Audrey Glover
Hubert Henry Goddard
Mr P Gough
Mr P Gough
John Greenhalgh
Mr Jonathan Gregory
Frank Grice
Mr R O Griffiths
Brenda Margaret Hadley
Anthony Gordon Hales
Mr George Henry Hall
Mrs J M Hancock
Isabel Handbury
G M Hardman
M F Harker
Charles Harriman
Mr Cyril Harris
Mr J H Hawkins
Margaret Hawkins
Sheila Hawksworth

Mr H J Hayes
George Haywood
Evelyn Hill
Alan H Hind
Mrs C K Hobbs
Mr F T Hodgkinson
J L Holland
W E Hollingworth
W T Holmes
Mr F Hooton
Maureen Hopewell
Richard Sandy Hopkin
Mrs C Horrocks
Ann & Neville Hoskins
Edward Houghton
Neville A Huckerby
R L Hulsman
Mrs G R Hutton
D R Hustwayte
D R Hustwayte
H Hutchings
Donald Jackson
Elisabeth Anne Jackson
Mavis & Keith Jackson
Glennys Anne Johnson
Stephanie Johnstone
Mrs Maureen Jones
Sidney Whitehill Kelly
Alan & Marian Kelvey
Richard Neil Kirk
Christine Knight
Mr S Land
J D Langham
Mr E J Lawrence
Howard G Lawrence
Cllr Meredith & Mrs Wendy Lawrence
Derek P Lawson
Ken & Jessie Leech
Stanley Leatherland
Colin M Lightfoot
Neil Lewin
Bryan Lonsdale
Ray & Dorothy Loseby
A & J Lovatt
Valerie Ann McCauly
Ian James McClair
Eric Macdonald
Anthony Machin
John & Tony Mackness
John Malbon
Mr H A Maling
Mrs Sheila M Manners
Reginald Martin
Mr & Mrs S G Marks
David Marriott
Richard Marriott
Mr Colin Hedley Marshall
Paul Marshall
L F Martin
T J Martin
Mr & Mrs C Mathewson ISM
Mr H E Mettham
E & M Middleton

G Millband
Geoffrey Mills
R B Mills
Horace W Moore
Mr & Mrs Morley
Thelma & Ken Morley
Mrs Dorothy Morris
Mrs E A Morris
John & Lily Morris
John & Lily Morris
Robin M Morris
Eric Morrison
William George Munks
Margaret Murray
John Nassau
Leslie Naylor
Martin J Nelson
Mr Paul Robert Nesbitt
Ray Newnes
Nottingham High School
Nottinghamshire County Council Local Studies
    Library
Nottinghamshire County Council Local Studies
    Library
Nottinghamshire County Council Local Studies
    Library
Nottinghamshire County Council Local Studies
    Library
Nottinghamshire County Council Local Studies
    Library
Nottinghamshire County Council Local Studies
    Library
Nottinghamshire County Council Local Studies
    Library
Nottinghamshire County Council Local Studies
    Library
Nottinghamshire County Council Local Studies
    Library
Nottinghamshire County Council Local Studies
    Library
Nottinghamshire County Council Local Studies
    Library
Nottinghamshire County Council Local Studies
    Library
Nottinghamshire County Council Local Studies
    Library
Nottinghamshire County Council Local Studies
    Library
Nottinghamshire County Council Local Studies
    Library
Nottinghamshire County Council Local Studies
    Library
Nottinghamshire County Council Local Studies
    Library
Nottinghamshire County Council Local Studies
    Library
Nottinghamshire County Council Local Studies
    Library
J E Osborne

Dorothy G O'Connor
B O'Sullivan
Robert Otter
Deryk J Page
Michael Paine
(née) Joyce Phyllis Payne
Colin John Pearce
Michael Peck
Alan Perry
Roy Plumb
Sue & Jack Poyner (Isle of Wight)
Mrs M E Price
Mrs K Prickard
David Alan Priestley
Mr & Mrs S T Pritchett
Stewart & Gillian Pygott
Lawrence J Quail
B Radmall
Doris Rawson
Kath & Snowy Read
Kenneth J Reddington
Susie M Reed
Mrs Ivy Reeves
Donald Reynolds
Charles Geoffrey Rhodes
Mr E Richardson
Mr F Richardson
Mrs L M Richardson
Mrs L M Richardson
Mrs Ruth E Richardson
D Ridgway
Anne (Scarborough) Rigley
Mr E Roebuck
D W Rook
M W Rossiter
G G Rothwell
Mr A Routway
C W Russell
Leslie Russell
Keith Scott
William V Sedgwick
Linda Sharpe
M A Shaw
Anne Shipman
Denise & Margaret Shirley
Margaret & David Sibley (Bingham)
Mr H Simpson
Elizabeth Mary Singer
George H Sleaford
Ray Sleaford
Cissie Smith
J H Smith
W W Snaith
Margaret Snellgrove
Walter Spencer
Cyril L Spridgeon
R W Squires
Mr Anthony Stephens
P R Stapleton
George Stevens
Christine Stevenson
Lewis K Stockdale
Mr W Storer

Arthur Sunderland
Mr Timothy Stubbs
F E W Swann
Harry Swann
T B Swanson (USA)
Mr Ronald Tansley
K W Tantum
David J Taverner (USA)
A R Taylor
Roy Leslie Taylor
John Tennick
G F & A J Terry
A C Thomas
F M Thompson
James A Tillson
W A Towers
John William Trent
John William Trent
John William Trent
David G Tutin
Mr E S Tutin
George Wallace Tye
C A Tyler
Charles Joseph Uttley
Mrs Rhoda Vaites
Edmund Frederick Varney
Michael Vaughan
Mr Michael Vickers
Mr Terrence Vickers
Albert E Walker
Mrs P Walker
Mrs C Wallis
Mr S I Walters
Mrs Dorothy Ward
Mr James Ward
Harold Warren
Terence Weatherbed
Sheila Welch
S O Westmoreland
Helen Westray-Cawthan
John & Sheila Wharton
Mr E P White
Michael J Whiting
Mr & Mrs K G Whiting
Mr & Mrs K G Whiting
Ellen Whittlesey
Mrs F M Wicks
Liam Michael Wilcox
Shirley & Ken Williams (Clifton)
S R Williams
Bernard Willis
B S Willis
Keith Winter
Georgine Wood
Maureen Woodward
P A Woodward
Robin & Jean Woolley
Joan Woolsey
B Woonton
J Worley
Heather Wroblewski
Alan & Elaine Yeo